What people are saying about "Struggling Under the Broom Tree"

"Struggling Under the Broom Tree" might seem like a quick read at first glance, but don't be fooled by its size. This is one of those books you'll prefer to pause and ponder with every paragraph. Bill shares the account of Elijah's lowest low along with his own. Also, like Elijah, Bill's story doesn't end under a broom tree. Despair is overcome at the cross."
- *Pastor Terry Michaels, Calvary Austin*

Pastor Bill is the real deal; a godly man, true friend, and surrendered servant. As you read through this book you will get to know him, especially as he shares some of his most raw moments as he wrestled with depression. Yes, Christians deal with depression, even pastors. But God is faithful, and He will meet you in your deepest need. You can trust Pastor Bill to take you to the Word, and to the God of the Word. Encouragement for you is just up ahead!
- *Ed Taylor, Pastor & Author, edtaylor.org*

In this book, I'm so amazed by the way Pastor Bill connects the Old Testament hero of the faith, Elijah with the challenges we face in everyday life. I love the way he describes real circumstances and trials in his life to connect us to Elijah, and ultimately point us to Christ. The Christian life is meant to be victorious, and yet so many people can relate with Elijah sitting under the broom tree. This book will challenge you to know Jesus in a deeper, more personal way. It will challenge you to seek the only One who can change your circumstances.

- *Ben Martinez, Calvary Chapel Lubbock*

In "Struggling Under the Broom Tree" you will read the testimony of my friend Pastor Bill Gehm. A testimony that reflects the real and genuine struggles that he has been through that make him who he is today. Far more importantly however is the real and genuine way Jesus revealed Himself to Bill in his times of greatest struggle, despair and depression. It is who Jesus is and how He changed Bill that really make Bill who he is that is at the core of this book. Are you depressed dear one? Are you overwhelmed with the situations and circumstances of life and wonder if God is there and aware of your troubles? Then read this book and be reassured once again that He is, He cares deeply for you, and He loves you with His perfect love. In reading this book I have been encouraged and I know you will be also, knowing that the same God who rescued Elijah and my friend Bill, will also rescue you and me. May God richly bless you!

- *Mike Nasci, Calvary Chapel Estancia Valley*

Struggling Under the Broom Tree

GOD'S RESCUE PLAN FOR DISCOURAGEMENT

By Bill Gehm
with Angela Gray

Summary: A study of the life of Elijah, and how God's faithfulness to him in the circumstances of his life brought him out from under the broom tree of despair.

ISBN number 978-0-578-33043-3

Published by Word Implanted in Amarillo, TX. All rights reserved.

Designed and printed by C&B Marketing, Amarillo, TX

PRINTED IN THE USA

I'd like to dedicate this book to Dennis Clounch –
my brother in Christ, mentor, father-figure,
and dear friend.
God used him to help pull me out from
under the broom tree many times in the past 30 years.
Dennis prayed prayers that seemed impossible –
and God answered them.
He is the most gracious and optimistic man
I have ever known.
I am forever thankful for you Dennis.
I love you.

Table of Contents

Foreword

I'm not sure where I would be had it not been for Pastor Bill and his transparency concerning his relationship with Jesus. Serving alongside Pastor Bill has been the best thing for me in both my walk with Jesus and my role as a pastor here in Galveston. Bill's time(s) spent under the broom tree has taught me that all leaders can end up underneath those branches, however, effective leaders learn from time spent there and allow the Lord to minister to them during those moments. The practical examples that Pastor Bill lays out in this book are ones that I have seen him live out, and they have also proven to be most effective in my journey. My prayer is that this book will remove any shame associated with "broom tree" experiences, and maybe more importantly how Jesus can both minister to and lead anyone out from underneath the shade of the broom tree.

James Grizzle, Calvary Chapel Galveston

Acknowledgements

I am so grateful to Angela Gray for the countless hours and dedication she poured into transcribing and writing this book. She truly made this happen.

Special thanks to:

My niece & Secretary, Mary, who helped to coordinate this project.

Ric Vogelgesang Scott Davey, and Dennis Clounch – who put their money where their mouth is!

My dear wife Cindy, who has lived with me too many times while I'm under the broom tree. She is the joy of my life.
I love you sweetie.

Grace Church – my family, my flock.

Most of all my Lord and Savior, who continues to rescue me and gives me fresh vision and hope.

I truly am a blessed man.

Introduction

"Forever, O Lord, Your word is settled in heaven."
Psalm 119:89

I've spent most of my life studying and preaching God's Word. Not once have I questioned whether or not it is the truth. It is eternally true. It has always been true, even before the first page of the Bible was written down. *"In the beginning was the Word, and the Word was with God, and the Word was God. He was in the beginning with God."(John 1:1-2)*

It was settled long ago - by God's command - that He would make man in His image. *"All things were made through Him, and without Him nothing was made that was made." (John 1:3).* It was settled long ago that *"God so loved the world that He gave His only begotten Son, that whoever believes in Him should not perish but have everlasting life." (John 3:16)* It was settled long ago that Jesus, the Son of God, would be *"...slain from the foundation of the world." (Revelation 13:8)* It was settled long ago that He would make me in His image, and that I would be chosen *"...before the foundation of the world, that we should be holy and without blame before Him in love, having predestined us to the adoption as sons by Jesus Christ to Himself, according to the good pleasure of His will, to the praise of the glory of His grace,*

by which He made us accepted in the Beloved."
(Ephesians 1:4-6)

I'm not only convinced of its everlasting truth, but as the years pass, I grow more confident in its *immediate* importance. Sometimes people ask me, "How can an ancient book written thousands of years ago possibly hold any significance to my life here and today?"

For me, the answer is obvious, but I know that no matter how many different ways I answer their question, it will never hold meaning for anyone until they discover *the Answer* for themselves. How, when, why, and where will never make sense until they understand **Who.** *"In Him was life, and the life was the light of men. And the light shines in the darkness, and the darkness did not comprehend it." (John 1:4-5)*

Instead of trying to answer the question, "Why should I care?" I steer them towards Someone who cares so much for them! The Word of God reveals God's nature, His will, and His character. Jesus Christ is the embodiment of that Word, and everything centers around Him. He is the Word of God made flesh. *"And the Word became flesh and dwelt among us, and we beheld His glory, the glory as of the only begotten of the Father, full of grace and truth." (John 1:14)*

His Word is eternal, settled, and unchanging, but it's more than that. The Word of God lives and breathes because it's written by the living, breathing God; as current and active today as it was when the words *"Let there be light"* gave birth to our existence. *"For the word of God is living and powerful, and sharper than any two-edged sword, piercing even to the division of soul and spirit, and of joints and marrow, and is a discerner of the thoughts and intents of the heart."* (Hebrews 4:12)

His Word set everything in motion, and it is the only thing that will stand forever. *"Heaven and earth will pass away, but My words will by no means pass away."* (Matthew 24:35)

But, I know that unless people meet the risen Savior for themselves, the Word of God will never come alive for them. I also know that when their eyes, their ears, their hearts, and their lives are opened to Jesus, they discover the meaning for their lives – to have a relationship with the God Who loves them. They discover the purpose for their lives – to share the Good News about Jesus with the people around them. They discover principles upon which to build their marriages, their families, their businesses, their finances – everything.

God's Word shows us the way. Jesus is the Way. God's Word shows us the truth. Jesus is the Truth. God's Word is alive. Jesus is the Life. When people meet the Lord Jesus, they answer the question for themselves.

*How can the Word of God **not** be relevant to our lives, here and now?!*

I am as excited to study and preach today as I was the first time. It's a sacred privilege with which God has entrusted me, and I do not take His call for granted.

"Blessed is the man
Who walks not in the counsel of the ungodly,
Nor stands in the path of sinners,
Nor sits in the seat of the scornful;
But his delight is in the law of the Lord,
And in His law he meditates day and night."
(Psalm 1:1-2)

Most of the people who are reading this book are part of the "blessed people". We've already embraced God's Word for the treasure that it is. We rest in the comfort of the Psalms. We incorporate Godly wisdom from the Proverbs. We rejoice in the Good News of the Gospels. We celebrate the birth of the church in Acts. We receive the counsel and pastoral instruction offered by Paul and the other apostles in their letters to the church. We've met the Author of the Bible. We hang on every word. We delight in His Word and we think on it day and night. We know that the Bible is the best way to live.

Preface

The People of the Bible

Are you discouraged? What does the Word say? Do you struggle with doubt, anger, sin? What does the Word say?

It all sounds simple doesn't it? We know where to go...The Word. We know upon whom to call...Jesus. So, why does it become so difficult to do sometimes?

The Bible reveals God to us – He is loving, good, merciful, holy, perfect, strong. God's Word shows us an eternal Kingdom – a kingdom to which we belong but have not yet seen – with a King who has taken up residence in our hearts. However, we still live in a fallen world with an enemy who roams about seeking out those he can devour. We are free from the penalty of sin and dead to the power of our sinful nature, but the presence of sin is still with us, and our flesh constantly fights to be resurrected. Our flesh is at war with the Spirit of God.

The contrast between God and man is so striking that sometimes it can leave us feeling hopeless. We love the Lord. We want to follow Him. We embrace His Word, but in spite of our best efforts, we fall short. The Apostle Paul understood the struggle so well that he was able to articulate perfectly the conflict that dwells within the man or woman of God.

"For I know that in me (that is, in my flesh) nothing good dwells; for to will is present with me, but how to perform what is good I do not find. For the good that I will to do, I do not do; but the evil I will not to do, that I practice. Now if I do what I will not to do, it is no longer I who do it, but sin that dwells in me. I find then a law, that evil is present with me, the one who wills to do good. For I delight in the law of God according to the inward man. But I see another law in my members, warring against the law of my mind, and bringing me into captivity to the law of sin which is in my members. O wretched man that I am! Who will deliver me from this body of death? I thank God - through Jesus Christ our Lord!"(Romans 7:18-25a)

This struggle is nothing new. It was present from the beginning, and it will follow us until God takes us to Heaven. The Good News is we are overcomers. Paul overcame his struggle through Jesus Christ! We're surrounded by a host of believers who came before us and have gone on to be with the Lord. They overcame, and so will we as long as we keep our eyes where they belong...on the Lord!

"...we are surrounded by so great a cloud of witnesses…" (Hebrews 12:1)

OK, Pastor Bill, but this is a book about Elijah. What does Elijah have to do with anything? He is an Old Testament figure who lived thousands of years ago.

It's easy to think of these men and women as

characters in a story rather than people who really lived and walked with God. Consequently, it can be hard to relate to these "legends of the faith". The name Elijah conjures up images of a strong man with a long beard and strange clothes, standing on top of a mountain, proclaiming the Word of the Lord, and calling down fire. It's true. He did all of that, but the book of James let us in on a secret about Elijah. *"Elijah was a man with a nature like ours,..." (James 5:17a),* and there was a time when he cowered in fear. He struggled with doubt and depression. He wanted to give up. He wasn't a super human. He simply served an amazing God.

The lives of these men and women are in there for a reason. They serve as practical illustrations of the truths we cling to. God is loving, merciful, compassionate, and enduring. He is slow to anger. He is faithful to His servants when they stand and fight, and He is still faithful when they stumble and want to quit. He isn't against us. Not at all. He is for us. He is patient with us. He leads, guides, and transforms us. He carries us when we get weary. He pulls us back on the narrow path with His gentle yoke when we try to go our own way. The Old Testament "heroes of the Bible" illustrate that beautifully. Elijah's life illustrates that beautifully.

Chapter 1

Elijah - The Man on Fire

I've studied and preached God's Word for forty years. Some of the people in the Bible have become my friends. I feel like I know them personally, and Elijah is one of my best friends. I identify with his personality and his ministerial approach. God used his story to influence my life and shape my ministry.

Who was Elijah? Where did he come from?

Elijah was a Tishbite. That's all we know about him. Was he from an important family? No one knows. Elijah burst onto the scene, seemingly out of nowhere, when he busted into King Ahab's court.

"And Elijah the Tishbite, of the inhabitants of Gilead, said to Ahab, 'As the Lord God of Israel lives, before whom I stand, there shall not be dew nor rain these years, except at my word.'"(1 Kings 17:1)

Elijah emerged from the shadows of obscurity as God placed him on the greatest stage in Israel to remind the people about the Living Lord God of Israel.

"And it came to pass, at the time of the offering of the evening sacrifice, that Elijah the prophet came near and said, 'Lord God of Abraham, Isaac, and Israel, let it be known this day that You are God in Israel and I am Your servant, and that I have done all

these things at Your word. Hear me, O Lord, hear me, that this people may know that You are the Lord God, and that You have turned their hearts back to you again.' Then the fire of the Lord fell and consumed the burnt sacrifice, and the wood and the stones and the dust, and licked up the water that was in the trench. Now when all the people saw it, they fell on their faces; and they said, 'The Lord, He is God! The Lord, He is God!'" (1 Kings 18:36-39)

Where we came from, who our family is; none of that matters. All that mattered was that Elijah was God's man; meticulously designed, ordained, and appointed to do a job. Elijah said, "Yes." Elijah got it done. He prayed, and God shut up the heavens. He prayed, and fire fell from Heaven. He prayed, and the rain came back.

In 1972 God busted into my life, seemingly out of nowhere. I was a sixteen year old boy who lived in a trailer park in Commerce City, Colorado. I was doing my own thing and going my own way when I literally crashed and burned. I flipped my motorcycle end over end down from the top of a hill to the bottom. I thought I was a dead man until I landed at the base of that hill and realized, "I'm still alive." I knew God spared my life so He could save my soul, and I stopped fighting Him. The dirt became my altar as I knelt down and cried, "Yes, Lord." I did die that day, but not in the way I thought I would. My old, sinful, good for nothing man stayed dead and buried, and from that miserable wreckage, I stood up and walked away, a brand new creation in Christ. I was God's man, meticulously designed, ordained, and appointed to do a job.

Almighty God drew up this amazing blueprint that encompasses eternity and expands into the infinite reaches of our universe because He is from everlasting to everlasting. Everything that exists is by His design. That in and of itself is beyond our ability to understand, but know this: contained within this brilliant Master Plan is a subset of plans, each one tailored to include our lives into this beautiful story that began before time and will continue long after Heaven and earth have passed away. This doesn't only apply to prophets like Elijah or to preachers like me. It isn't for a handful of elite believers. It's for all of us!

We're all saved by grace! We're all given the opportunity to decide whether or not we're going to follow, and the moment we say "yes" we become *"His workmanship, created in Christ Jesus for good works, which God prepared beforehand that we should walk in them." (Ephesians 2:10)*

Elijah was just a man. I am just a man. But, we serve the Almighty God, the Creator of everything. We all long for a life of significance, to know that our existence somehow made at least a small impact while we walked on this earth. We find that fulfillment in only one place, in service to the Kingdom of God.

Only one thing lasts forever, the Word of God. Only one Kingdom will last forever, the Kingdom of God. We were created in the image of God, for His good pleasure, to fulfill His design for our lives. We live to represent the Gospel of Jesus Christ. It all centers around the Lord Jesus Christ.

Great God, Great Message, Great Faith

Elijah, the Great Prophet of God, was a man with a *nature like ours (James 5:17),* living through some of Israel's most disheartening times. Corrupt leaders, wicked people, Godlessness – this is nothing new, and Elijah faced them all just like we do. Elijah had a wonderful message for the people of Israel. Jehovah is *still* God. He is *still Almighty* God, and He *still* longs to be their God. He was for His people. He wanted them to come back! Elijah knew the message. He knew the God behind the message, and he charged forward fearlessly declaring God's Word, emboldened by God's power. Elijah's allegiance to God's Word and his faith made him willing to follow wherever God sent him, which eventually led him to the top of Mount Carmel.

"Then the fire of the Lord fell and consumed the burnt sacrifice, and the wood and the stones and the dust, and it licked up the water that was in the trench. Now when all the people saw it, they fell on their faces; and they said, 'The Lord, He is God! The Lord,

He is God!'" (1 Kings 18:38-39)

Elijah became a vessel through which God could perform great exploits of His greatness and power. God was the source. Elijah was the vessel.

God called me to be a preacher, and He commissioned me to be the pastor of Grace Church in Amarillo, Texas. God united me, my wife, and seventeen other people to begin a church in a lock shop in 1985, and He has been as faithful to His Word with the work in our lives as He was to Elijah as he stood on Mount Carmel.

We were committed to God's Word. We had faith in God, and we were willing to follow wherever He sent us. God gave us a mountain too, the intersection of Western and Plains in Amarillo. Most of the Texas Panhandle is dry and flat, but Western and Plains is one of the highest points in my city. On that intersection stood an abandoned grocery store for sale, 112,000 square feet, and the moment I peered into the window of that building, I knew this was where God wanted us to stand and build a church! It is one of the busiest crossroads in town as people drive west toward the medical district, or south to catch I-40. God gave me a burden for that intersection; not for the building, but for every soul that drove through that intersection whether they travel north, south, east, or west.

We were ready for whatever God wanted to do on that mountain. We knew God was our source, and we knew we wanted to be the vessels!

"Now it happened in the meantime that the sky became black with clouds and wind, and there was a heavy rain. So Ahab rode away and went to Jezreel. Then the hand of the Lord came upon Elijah; and he girded up his loins and ran ahead of Ahab to the entrance of Jezreel." (1 Kings 18:45-46)

1 Kings 18 is the kind of day every preacher dreams of. Elijah stood atop Mount Carmel, declaring God's Word, watching God's fire fall, and witnessing the hearts of God's people repent. He outran a chariot in his victory lap!

God gave us the building! He gave us Radio By Grace! I had the greatest message on earth – the Good News – and I couldn't wait to declare it to the neighborhood, to my city, and to all across the country and even different parts of the world. It was more than I knew to even dream of when my wife and I rolled into Amarillo, TX in 1980. I thought to myself, "This is great! I'm doing what God called me to do. I'm stepping out in faith, so this shouldn't be too hard! What could go wrong now?"

The Revenge of an Enemy

"And Ahab told Jezebel all that Elijah had done, also how he had executed all the prophets with the sword. Then Jezebel sent a messenger to Elijah, saying, 'So let the gods do to me, and more also, if I do

*not make your life as the life of one of them by tomor-
row about this time.'"(1 Kings 19:1-2)*

Don't expect everyone to celebrate when the fire
falls and the rains come. On top of Mount Carmel,
Elijah forgot about his enemy who waited for him as
soon as he came back down – Jezebel. Jezzy was
the wicked wife of King Ahab, and she's the one who
really held the power in Israel. She wasn't about to
give up her hold on Israel without a fight. Jezzy's allegiance was to Baal, the supposed god of the sky, and
up until this point, she led Israel's heart away from
their true God and towards this impostor who had no
power at all.

Elijah made an enemy in Jezebel from that first
day he said, "Yes!" to God's commission to stand and
issue his proclamation that God would shut up the
skies and turn off the rains. The enemy of God placed
a target on Elijah's back. When she heard that Elijah
destroyed the false prophets of Baal and turned the
heart of Israel back to their one true God, her resolve
to destroy him only intensified!

I forgot about my enemy, the prince of the power
of the air, the enemy who opposed God and His
people, and as God advanced His Kingdom through
Grace Church, through radio, through us – the
enemy strengthened his resolve to take us out and
make us useless.

The Words of the Enemy

Don't underestimate the power of words. Proverbs 18 warns us that "Death and life are in the power of the tongue," with the strength to build up and to tear down. The enemy uses words like bullets from a gun. One word – an angry text or a scathing email – fired off at precisely the right time can inflict wounds that penetrate deeper and do more damage than a thousand lashes with a stick. Physical wounds hurt, but they heal. Hate-filled words wound the heart, soul, and spirit. Words kill our joy, and when joy fades our strength falters.

Men and women of God must carefully measure the words they speak and the words they listen to, filtering every one of them through the truth of the Word of God. Nothing good comes from listening to the enemy, but if we must listen or reply, put on the whole armor of God first. (Ephesians 6)

Elijah listened to the threats and the lies. This bold, larger-than-life prophet became afraid and discouraged. In his despair he forgot about the three years that God safely tucked him away from the threat of his enemy. He forgot about God's glorious provision with the ravens and the miracles he witnessed with the widow of Zarephath. He forgot about God's fiery display on Mount Carmel and the refreshing rain showers that revived Israel. Elijah became depressed, and in his desperation, he ran away and hid. For a brief time, Jezzy got exactly what she wanted. She got rid of the prophet that threatened her plans, her reign, and her kingdom.

I love 1 Kings 19. I love Elijah. I love that God told us the truth about him. He didn't always have it together. He didn't always stand and fight. He went from experiencing a great, faith-filled victory to being derailed by the words from his enemy. This great ancestor of our faith ran away.

I needed this story because not long after our church purchased our new building and we began climbing the mountain of radio, the enemy took aim and fired with the words I feared the most.

"You're broke. You have no money. You have nothing."

I didn't know how to respond. Fear took over and depression blindsided me like a cheap shot to the stomach. I couldn't stand, and I couldn't breathe. The only thing I knew to do was to run from everyone and hide.

I didn't understand it. I followed God! I knew I did. I dreamed about how God would use Grace Church at Western and Plains to change our city. I expected God to do His thing. I didn't expect the fierce opposition, and I surely didn't expect God to seemingly grow silent. All I heard were the whispers behind my back; people questioning my sanity, my integrity, my ego, and even my faith.

It was hard: hard to read my Bible, hard to pray, hard to preach to my congregation. I watched in distress as half of my congregation left for "greener pastures." The thought of facing even one more day overwhelmed me. My pride was wounded, my spirit was crushed, and my heart filled with despair. The joy was gone, and it left me weak. I entered into the worst season of depression in my life.

Nothing Hidden in the Fine Print

"That's not very spiritual, Pastor Bill. We're supposed to live by faith and not by sight."

Maybe it doesn't sound spiritual, but it's the truth. God never shied from telling us the truth, and Jesus despaired at the thought of what He was about to face on the cross. *"My soul is exceedingly sorrowful, even unto death." (Matthew 26:38)*

He pressed on, in faithfulness to His purpose, but every step grew more and more painful as the burden of the cross, the burden of our sin grew heavier.

The Gospel centers around Jesus Christ! Jesus Christ overcame! Jesus Christ defeated the enemy! Yes! All true, and one day every knee will bow and give Him His due as King of kings and Lord of lords – but the first time Jesus came to this earth, He had to suffer. He also warned us that if we really want to follow Him, we would have to suffer too. If we want to share in His glory, we have to share in His suffering.

It's in black and white. He hid nothing in the fine print. *"In the world you will have tribulation;" (John 16:33).* Trials, testing, temptations; they are all part of the package, and sometimes they are agonizing. To become the Conquering King, Jesus first had to become the Man of Sorrows, enduring the cross, in order to save the people He loved so deeply. Praise God it doesn't end there. *"...but be of good cheer, I have overcome the world."* He did! He defeated sin, hell, and the grave.

It ends well! I know we know this. It's so easy to say, but sometimes it's difficult to hold onto, especially in the death grip of our worst trials. The ending seems far away, but the pain hurts now!

Chapter 2

The Broom Tree

"And when he saw that, he arose and ran for his life, and went to Beersheba, which belongs to Judah, and left his servant there. But he himself went a day's journey into the wilderness, and came and sat down under a broom tree. And he prayed that he might die, and said, 'It is enough! Now, Lord, take my life, for I am no better than my fathers!'" (1 Kings 19:3-4)

God was on Elijah's side. The words of a wicked witch could never derail the plans of God, and He wasn't finished with Elijah, not by a long shot, but somewhere between 1 Kings 17 and 1 Kings 19 Elijah started listening to the wrong voice.

Jezebel threatened, "I'm going to kill you!" Elijah prayed, "Take my life now, God!"

The enemy masterfully disguises his voice as our own. I internalized what people were saying about me, and started telling myself, "You *are* a fool. You *are* a failure." The fear of failing leveled me, and I couldn't even endure my staff meetings. Nothing seemed to work; no Bible verses, no pats on the back.

Once or twice I literally hid under my desk.

Elijah hid under his broom tree.

The enemy didn't have to take us out. We took ourselves out; sidelined by fear and discouragement.

But, there was one thing we both got right. We both poured out our hearts to God. Deep down I think we both knew that God still cared for us, so we prayed. The good news is that God was still for us. The enemy was against us, but not God. God is always *for* His people, and He heard our prayers.

He already had angels ready to dispatch to minister to Elijah in his weakened state. God already had men and women in my life ready to minister to my most vulnerable places, and who knows what went on in the unseen realm of the supernatural on my behalf. God always works on behalf of His people – always – through His people, through His angels, and through Himself. I couldn't see Him or feel Him then, but looking back now, I see it all so clearly, and I am thankful to the God who hears all of our prayers; our faith-filled shouts of victory, and our desperate whispers for help.

Touched by an Angel

"Then as he lay and slept under a broom tree, suddenly an angel touched him, and said to him, "Arise and eat." Then he looked, and there by his head was a cake baked on coals, and a jar of water. So he ate and drank, and lay down again." (1 Kings 19:5-6)

God's plans didn't include leaving Elijah to die. God's plans included taking Elijah up in a whirlwind. Elijah would never die, but he didn't know that yet. For Elijah to start moving again, he needed healing in his body, soul, and spirit. The Great Physician started by ministering to Elijah's physical body.

Ministering to the physical needs of those who have been derailed, for whatever reason, is as sacred as ministering to their souls. Jesus explained it like this. *" ... 'for I was hungry and you gave Me food; I was thirsty and you gave Me drink; I was a stranger and you took Me in; I was naked and you clothed Me; I was sick and you visited Me; I was in prison and you came to Me.'' Then the righteous will answer Him, saying, 'Lord, when did we see You hungry and feed You, or thirsty and give You drink? When did we see You a stranger and take You in, or naked and clothe You? Or when did we see You sick, or in prison, and come to You?' And the King will answer and say to them, 'Assuredly, I say to you, inasmuch as you did it to one of the least of these My brethren, you did it to Me.'" (Matthew 25:35-40)*

God uses people like angels, and they minister all through my church. When someone finds themselves under a broom tree for whatever reason, they dispatch themselves immediately; running errands, bringing meals, doing household chores. It's amazing how much simply caring for the physical needs of those who are temporarily taken out by circumstances can encourage someone to face another day.

Elijah poured out his heart to his God, then laid down to rest. He was too weak to stand. The enemy stole his joy, and Elijah lost his strength. The first angel ministered to Elijah, making sure he had what he needed before he laid down to rest again. *One breath at a time, Elijah,* and that is an important step when circumstances knock us down. The Lord provides and sustains during those times.

We are the body, that's true; and God uses men and women, during key times in a person's life, to help them hang on until the next day.

The Touch of the Lord

"And the angel of the Lord came back the second time, and touched him, and said, 'Arise and eat, because the journey is too great for you.'" (1 Kings 19:7)

As Elijah slept, the Bible records another Angel Who ministered to him. The "Lord" is capitalized in this verse. Most scholars assert that this was a possible pre-incarnate manifestation of Jesus. This Angel was in a different category. God's faithfulness reaches far beyond our failures, and He does not toss us aside; not when we are weak or discouraged, not when we fail, and not even when we sin. Therefore, we must get back up and start moving again, and we can't do that in our own strength or willpower.

Praise God for those ministering angels, but that isn't enough. We need the touch of the Lord.

Elijah still had a long way to go, and for him to complete the journey, he needed the touch of the Lord

Jesus Himself. Elijah couldn't pick himself back up, no matter how much he wanted to. Praise God that this Angel of the Lord reached down when Elijah couldn't reach up, and gave him the strength he needed for the rest of the journey to come. God's plans for Elijah didn't end with Mount Carmel.

My depression swallowed me whole, and I thought I was drowning. I couldn't breathe. Not even my wife knew what to do. There was nothing she could do. I needed the Light of Jesus. I needed the personal touch of my Savior.

One day the phone rang at the church office, and my secretary answered. She informed the caller, "I'm sorry, but the pastor is hiding under his desk!" That day, I really was.

On the other end of that phone was my friend Steve Atkins from California, who oversaw radio stations all across the country. He was reading through a list of churches when my name jumped off the page at him. God instructed him, "Call Bill Gehm." As we spoke, I felt the soothing comfort of the Holy Spirit. Shortly thereafter, my good friend Billy Hobbs from San Antonio, called and assured me, "You're not crazy!"

I didn't know God could sound like Steve Atkins or Billy Hobbs, and I didn't know how to pick myself back up – but God did! I couldn't reach high enough, so God reached down low enough. *"He sent from above,*

He took me; He drew me out of many waters. He delivered me from my strong enemy, from those who hated me, for they were too strong for me." (Psalm 18:16-17)

Jesus still reaches down to us. He did what none other could do. *"For when we were still without strength, in due time Christ died for the ungodly." (Romans 5:6)* No one else could rescue us from the pit of sin; not our loved ones, not our religious organizations, not even the angels of Heaven. We all needed the hand of the Lord, and He provided for us. Jesus said, *"Take, eat; this is My body. Drink... all of you. For this is My blood of the new covenant, which is shed for many for the remission of sins." (Matthew 26:26-28)* Jesus provides everything we need to revive and sustain us for the long journey; from the depths of sin to our Heavenly rest with God the Father. God prepares a table for us in the presence of our enemies. He restores our souls. He leads us and transforms us from glory to glory. He sustains us until we reach Mount Zion where we will dwell in His house forever.

However, it wasn't time for Elijah to go to Heaven...not yet. Elijah's life wasn't over. Be sure that He who began the good work. .. He will finish it! God's plans for Elijah didn't end when he came off of Mount Carmel. The touch of Jesus empowered Elijah to stand up and start moving forward again so that He could complete what He wanted to do in Elijah's life.

The touch of Jesus through Steve Atkins and Billy Hobbs gave me strength to stand up and keep moving forward. I still struggled. The battle wasn't over, but I knew that God heard my prayers. He still had my back. Elijah couldn't give up on God because God didn't give up on him. I couldn't give up on God because He didn't give up on me.

God remembers that we're human. There's a reason we call it "amazing grace!" *"But we have this treasure in earthen vessels, that the excellence of the power may be of God and not of us. We are hard-pressed on every side, yet not crushed; we are perplexed, but not in despair; persecuted, but not forsaken; struck down, but not destroyed – always carrying about in the body the dying of the Lord Jesus, that the life of Jesus also may be manifested in our body. For we who live are always delivered to death for Jesus' sake, that the life of Jesus also may be manifested in our mortal flesh." (2 Corinthians 4:7-11)*

It was God's idea to partner with these weak vessels! He works through us in the middle of our weaknesses and failures. He uses us in spite of our weaknesses and failures. Sometimes, He uses us because of our weaknesses and failures because He alone receives the glory.

"These things I have spoken to you, that in Me you may have peace. In the world you will have tribulation;

but be of good cheer, I have overcome the world."
(John 16:33)

Get back up! Start moving! As long as there is breath, there is hope because God isn't finished yet!

Chapter 3

Man on Fire: The Flame Restored
A New Hope; a New Mountain

The heroes of the Bible were no different from us; and God is still the same God. He reveals His strength in our weakness. He displays His wisdom in our foolishness. I don't know how that works, but it does, and we're able to comfort others because we know the God who comforts us in all of our tribulations.

Perhaps Elijah wishes God would have skipped 1 Kings 19, because humanly speaking, it wasn't Elijah's finest hour. I, for one, am glad God did include this season because God used it to comfort me when I found myself under the broom tree. I needed to see the God of all comfort in Elijah's life, and God places people in our own lives who need to experience that same comfort.

The "iron man" of the Old Testament wasn't the only hero of faith to suffer. The Apostle Paul was the "iron man" of the New Testament. Paul penned two-thirds of the New Testament; he saw the Third heaven; he was imprisoned for the Gospel, and he wrote these words: *"For we do not want you to be ignorant, brethren, of our trouble which came to us in Asia: that we were burdened beyond measure, above strength, so that we despaired even of life. Yes, we had the sentence of death in ourselves, that we should not trust in ourselves but in God who raises the dead, who delivered us from so great a death, and does deliver us; in whom we trust that He will still deliver us, you also helping together in prayer for us, that thanks may be given by many persons on our behalf for the gift granted to us through many." (2 Corinthians 1:8-11)*

The Bible uses the Greek word *exaporeo* in this passage, which means to be utterly at a loss, without hope or resources, destitute. Living was too painful, so they trusted in the God who raises the dead. He had delivered them. He was still delivering them. He would continue to deliver them into His hands and His care.

Another iron man of the New Testament, John the Baptist, came in the spirit of Elijah to prepare the way for Jesus. He baptized Jesus and literally heard the voice of God the Father say, *"This is My Beloved Son in Whom I am well pleased."* John saw the truth with his own eyes, heard it with his own ears, touched it with his hands, and proclaimed it with his mouth. However, when he was thrown into prison... he doubted, and he questioned, *"Are You the Coming One, or do we look for another?" (Matthew 11:2-3).* Jesus simply reminded him, *"The blind see and the lame walk; the lepers are cleansed and the deaf hear;*

the dead are raised up and the poor have the gos-pel preached to them." (Matthew 11:4-5) John did remember, and despite the fear and despair, John followed Jesus to the death. Momentary doubt didn't undo his faith, and Jesus Himself commended John as the greatest born of a woman. (Matthew 11:11; Luke 7:28)

My point is this. Godly people struggle with depression, despair, doubt, and fear, but God's grace meets us in the midst of those struggles. He met me under the desk just like He met me under the motor-cycle. He didn't leave me alone to die. He delivered me then, and He delivers me now. I know tough times are ahead, but I also know that same God will deliver me, no matter where I find myself.

The Great Physician's Orders
Rest

"Then as he lay and slept under a broom tree..." (1 Kings 19:5)

Included in God's blueprint for working, is a pro-vision for rest. He worked six days and rested on the seventh. Why did He do that? He's the God who never slumbers, but He built in rest for us. Work six days; rest one day.

Lack of rest leads to burn out. Burn out leads to depression. Depression leads to quitting.

I made myself build one day of Sabbath rest into

my schedule; one day a week when I rest my body, soul, and mind. My rest is sacred because it is essential to the longevity of my ministry.

I don't have a television in my bedroom – though I do have a ton of books on my night stand. I want to fill my mind with "God thoughts" that will make their way into my heart as I drift off to sleep. Two metal slats in my bedroom window form a cross. I didn't plan on that! In the middle of that window, my wife place the letters J O Y. When I can't sleep, I look up at that window. I see the cross, and I see J O Y. I've created a cave, a hiding place with God. I never want to be under the desk again, and making sure I rest is part of my prescription from God. Rest is holy! God created Sabbath rest for man.

Physical Touch

"...suddenly an angel touched him..." (1 Kings 19:5)
There is something special about when the Lord reaches down to touch us. He still does that today. We feel His touch on our lives and in our hearts.

God also uses His church to be His hands and feet. For some people, church is the only place where they can receive that simple "touch" of connection. They don't feel so alone. Part of Elijah's problem was that he felt like he was all alone and nobody understood.

In the middle of my depression I attended a

Calvary Chapel Pastor's Conference. Those men of God sensed that I needed extra support. Those brothers laid their hands on my shoulder or gave me a quick hug. Some of them prayed over me. That extra connection ministered to my wounded soul.

I realize the subject of touch is tricky, especially in today's society. Use discernment; whether or not they need a handshake, or a quick hug, or a pat on the shoulder. Sometimes, they simply need someone to sit with them. We should use caution and be sensitive to the Holy Spirit's leading, but don't be afraid to establish physical connection with hurting people. Jesus never shied away from anyone; not the lepers, or the diseased, or the woman with the issue of blood, or even a dead girl, and His touch always brought healing and restoration.

Slow Down

"So he arose, and ate and drank; and he went in the strength of that food forty days and forty nights as far as Horeb, the mountain of God." (1 Kings 19:8)

Most scholars agree that God led Elijah to the same mountain where He communed with Moses. I don't believe for a second that it was by coincidence. God knew where He was leading Elijah. Mount Horeb was about a fifteen-day journey from the broom tree, so why did it take forty days to get there? Elijah needed to slow down. God raised Elijah back to his feet, and Elijah moved forward, one step at a time, until one step at a time turned into full on scaling the mountain. Walking with God often looks like that, leading us step by step, and we don't recognize the progress He has made with us until we stop and look around at how far we have traveled, or how high we have climbed.

I take my time in our church services. People "counsel" me that if we trim our services down to one hour, more people would attend. However, I would rather slow down with sheep who are well fed, well cared for, and on pace with God, even if that means I have a smaller church. We still have Wednesday night services so that during the middle of a trying week, we can come together, slow down, catch our breath, and commune with God.

Our *relationship* with God is more important than the work we do for Him. The work will get done when we are in relationship with Him because our work is the overflow of our relationship. He breathes in, and we breathe out. The more we commune with God, the less we find ourselves under the broom tree.

God's Rehab

"And there he went into a cave, and spent the night in that place;" (1 Kings 19:9a)

It's amazing how quickly we turn to our own human strength to solve spiritual struggles. We made the mess, now we want to clean it up, or we want to hide from it. Adam and Eve did their best to conceal their shame by hiding, and they covered themselves with the garments they made from leaves, but it was inadequate for covering and protection. God stepped in and covered them with the garments He fashioned.

Elijah had his own idea of shelter under the broom tree, but it fell short. It had no protection from the sun or weather, and it had no protection from an enemy who still wanted to kill him. God led Elijah into a cave where He could safely tuck him away with only one way in and one way out. It was likely the same cleft in the rock where Moses hid as God's glory passed by. (Exodus 33).

I created my own idea of refuge, but I wasn't safely hidden away. My enemy still knew where to find me. I was overwhelmed, and I didn't want to admit how much I needed help, how inadequate I was to do this on my own. This life sends some intense storms our way. Our enemy hurls as many fiery darts as he can. We can't stand on our own. We need the shelter of our Rock, the Rock of Christ Jesus. He is the only way in and the only way out, and our enemies cannot get past Him.

When I am overwhelmed, lead me to the Rock that is higher than I. *"He who dwells in the secret place of the Most High shall abide under the shadow of the Almighty. I will say of the Lord, 'He is my refuge*

and my fortress; My God, in Him I will trust.'" (Psalm
91:1-2)

> A wonderful Savior is Jesus my Lord,
>   a wonderful Savior to me;
> He hideth my soul in the cleft of the rock,
>   where rivers of pleasure I see
> He hideth my soul in the cleft of the rock,
> That shadows a dry, thirsty land;
> He hideth my life in the depths of His love,
> And covers me there with His hand,
> And covers me there with His hand.
> (Hymn - He Hideth My Soul)

A Heart to Heart Talk with God

"...and behold, the word of the Lord came to him,
and He said to him, 'What are you doing here, Elijah?'
So he said, 'I have been very zealous for the Lord
God of hosts; for the children of Israel have forsaken
Your covenant, torn down Your altars, and killed Your
prophets with the sword. I alone am left; and they
seek to take my life.'"(1 Kings 19:9b-10)

Life moves fast, and situations can change with
the next breath we take or the next phone call we
receive. Elijah tumbled from the top of Mount Carmel
into the valley of depression in just a matter of hours.
Those things that sideline us – tragedies, our own
sin, attacks of the enemy, failing a test of faith –
all of those things make it easy to crawl in a hole

somewhere and nurse our wounds.

"What are you doing here, Elijah?"

God didn't give up on Elijah. No! God made the first move. Elijah needed one on one time with God. He invited Elijah in; into the cave where He would reveal Himself as well as minister to Elijah's wounded heart. Elijah felt like a failure. He felt like God let him down; that God no longer cared. He felt abandoned by everyone, especially God.

God wants a two-way conversation with His people. We call it prayer. He wants it so much that He allowed His Son to die, sealing the chasm that separated man from God. He paid a high price for it.

The only way for poisonous roots – doubt, fear, confusion, anger, disappointment, bitterness (even whon directed towards God) to be dug up and removed is to open our hearts to Him in prayer and allow Him access to our deepest spaces.

"What are you doing here Bill?"

I didn't yell at God in a cave. I stood in the middle of what would one day be my church's sanctuary, and I yelled, "I did what You said! I'm all in, but it's not working! I'm losing, my church is losing, and it looks like You're losing! I've been in Your corner since I was sixteen, so where are You now?"

One of the Godliest men I know, one of my best friends, lost his 26-year-old son to a heart attack he suffered while mowing his yard. He admitted to me that he has a hard time praying for his surviving children because he remembers how hard he prayed for his oldest boy. He's a faithful pastor, zealous for the Lord. He prayed, and he prayed in faith, yet his son still died. He still wants to know why.

It's OK to ask, "Why?" Jesus did. Jesus felt forsaken by His Father. He cried out, *"My God, my God, why have You forsaken me?"* Jesus is the perfect intercessor because he does understand.

God remembers we're human. God *invited* Elijah into the cave. He didn't kick him out. God didn't strike me down in my sanctuary. He met me there. God didn't disqualify my friend from the ministry because he struggled with reconciling what he couldn't understand with what he knew to be truth. God remained close and gave him the strength to keep going.

The Good News is that we have an advocate with God the Father. *"For we do not have a High Priest who cannot sympathize with our weaknesses, but was in all points tempted as we are, yet without sin. Let us therefore come boldly to the throne of grace, that we may obtain mercy and find grace to help in time of need." (Hebrews 4:15-16)* Our High Priest understands because He has been there, and He overcame. Nothing, and I mean nothing, can separate us from God's love. We have one on one face time with Almighty God because we are tucked away in Christ Jesus.

I descended into the darkness of depression, but the darkness could not overcome the Light of the Gospel. I remember the day God saved me. I remember the countless times God drew me in so He could whisper my name and pour the healing oil of His Spirit over me.

"What are you doing here?"

God never lost sight of Elijah. He doesn't lose sight of us either. No matter how bad it gets, the Gospel is still the Good News. The Kingdom of God is still coming. Nothing can stop the Word of the Lord. Nothing can stop Jesus, and a mountain is coming that we will never have to leave, Mount Zion. Jesus Christ will be revealed in all of His glory, and I know I will say, "It was worth it!" The struggles, the sorrows, the desk...all of it, because He is worth it. He is our prize.

Chapter 4

A New Revelation

"Then He said, 'Go out, and stand on the mountain before the Lord.' And behold, the Lord passed by, and a great and strong wind tore into the mountains and broke the rocks in pieces before the Lord, but the Lord was not in the wind; and after the wind an earthquake, but the Lord was not in the earthquake; and after the earthquake a fire, but the Lord was not in the fire; and after the fire a still small voice." (1 Kings 19:11-12)

Amarillo is one of the windiest cities in the nation. I've seen wind uproot trees, blow off roofs, and even overturn cars but I have never seen a wind so strong that it can break apart rocks. God is all powerful, and sometimes He does things loud! I like loud. The fire that fell on Mount Carmel was just a tiny peek behind a curtain that conceals a greatness that man can't begin to understand.

People always tell me, "If I could witness one tiny display of God's power, if I could see a miracle, then I would believe." God affirms His greatness everywhere. Romans 1 says we clearly see the invisible attributes of God in creation, and Psalm 19 reveals that the heavens declare the glory of God. The skies proclaim the work of His hands.

Jezebel could see, touch, and smell the rain as it

fell around her, but she hardened her heart. Israel witnessed more miracles than any other nation, including miracle after miracle by the Messiah, but it was not enough. They still hardened their hearts. The problem is not with the Lord. It's with our hearts.

The wind, earthquake, fire: those were manifestations of God's power. They were part of His creation. The gentle whisper was the voice of God; the Word of God. Nothing is more powerful than God's Word, even when it is present in a still small voice. Nothing can stand against God's Word; not winds or earthquakes, certainly not threats from a wicked witch, not even all the forces of hell. The power behind everything is God's Word.

"So it was, when Elijah heard it, that he wrapped his face in his mantle and went out and stood in the entrance of the cave. Suddenly a voice came to him, and said, 'What are you doing here, Elijah?'" (1 Kings 19:13)

Fires, earthquakes, the ability to break apart rocks and mountains .... that was Elijah's God, the One who stood beside him on Mount Carmel. With one snap of His fingers He could uproot and destroy anything or anyone who stood in His way. Jezebel could roar and roar. She could even bare her teeth, but God stood beside Elijah. He still had plans for Elijah and Israel, so Jezebel was already as good as defeated.

When God addressed Elijah, God was reaching

out to His friend. His voice was as gentle as a soft whisper, but it was filled with the same power that split the rocks. The power wasn't in the volume of God's voice, it was in the truth of the Words He spoke, verified by the Great I AM.

"Thy will be done."

Jesus turned the voice of surrender and sacrifice into the most powerful force of the ages, with the ability to destroy every work of the enemy and render every weapon of darkness useless. Jesus will return with a shout and a voice so powerful that it defeats every army that rises up against Him. That day is coming, but it's not here yet.

Right now, Jesus gently calls to us. *Come near and find rest for your burdened souls and protection from your fiercest enemies.*

I've watched the soft, loving voice of Jesus Christ pierce through the hardest of hearts and bring the toughest of men to their knees. The *kindness* of God leads to repentance, and when He calls us by name it changes everything!

God called Elijah by his name. Perhaps Elijah was overwhelmed by God's power, but we know he was overcome by His kindness. He hid his face and drew near to his Friend, his Ever-Present help. The God who brought down fire against His enemies sat with him in his cave of depression as a Friend.

God's glory and man's pride cannot exist in the

same space. Elijah yielded his pride, and his heart melted under God's Word, gentle as a whisper. God transformed Elijah's angry, stubborn heart into a humble heart of flesh. A humble heart becomes a soft heart. A soft heart becomes a repentant heart. A repentant heart becomes an open heart. An open heart becomes a transformed heart.

God never lost sight of me. He didn't forget my name. He knows everything about us, including the words we utter even before we have the thought to say them. Sometimes we catch a glimpse of His great power and His great love for us in the same place. It's overwhelming when we understand this great God cares about His servants. *"Who am I, O Lord God? And what is my house, that You have brought me this far?" (2 Samuel 7:18)*

Who am I, O Lord, that You would call me by name, that You would choose me, that You would bring me all this way, that You would be with me until the end of the age?

"And he said, 'I have been very zealous for the Lord God of hosts; because the children of Israel have forsaken Your covenant, torn down Your altars, and killed Your prophets with the sword. I alone am left; and they seek to take my life.'" (1 Kings 19:14)

Elijah opened his heart, but he still had questions. God listened to Elijah. He communed with Elijah, but God didn't explain Himself; not on the mountain, or at the broom tree, or even on Mount Carmel. He did reveal Himself. He was God. He was sovereign. He was faithful. He was good. Elijah found THE ANSWER. His answer was God, I AM.

Why do the wicked prevail? What is happening to our country? What if they kill us? Could our best days be behind us? We will always have questions, and they will never be answered to our satisfaction if we seek to know the answer by our own wisdom and understanding. The Apostle Peter wrote, *"Therefore humble yourselves under the mighty hand of God, that He may exalt you in due time, casting all your care upon Him, for He cares for you." (1 Peter 5:6-7)*

There is our answer. We cast all of our worries, all of the things we cannot understand on Him. He cares for us. We won't always understand. We don't have to understand. We have to trust. God revealed Himself in Jesus. Our God saves through Jesus. Jesus is our answer, our wisdom, our understanding, our resurrection, and our life. In Him we live and move and have our being.

The Big Picture

Elijah felt isolated...alone. We can't trust our feelings. Sometimes, we can't even trust our own senses. That is why the Bible instructs us over and over to trust in the Lord and not our understanding. Paul reminded us we walk by faith and not by sight. Elijah had never been alone. God was with him in every season, and Elijah was not the only one who stood for God.

While God hid Elijah by a brook and provided for him through a Gentile widow, there was another man left behind in the middle of Israel's drought. Obadiah witnessed the massacre of God's prophets. He watched God's people struggle and suffer from the effects of the drought that lingered on because the king of God's people refused to listen. Obadiah risked everything as he hid one hundred of God's prophets, fifty to a cave, and he provided for all of their needs. Obadiah didn't bow.

What about those one hundred prophets? They didn't bow either.

There was something Elijah didn't know.

"Yet I have reserved seven thousand in Israel, all whose knees have not bowed to Baal, and every mouth that has not kissed him." (1 Kings 19:18)

Elijah couldn't see the big picture, but God did. Mount Carmel wasn't the end of the story. It was God's story about God's people. Elijah was a great prophet, an important man, but he was only part of that story. Elijah's call was never just about himself. He understood this in the beginning. Elijah's life was about the Word of God and the people of God, but once he started listening to the enemy's lies and threats, his focus shifted inward. It's dangerous to look to ourselves. When we look to "Me, Myself, and I," we will run straight back to the broom tree. We were never meant to live for ourselves.

Jesus set His face upwards to God His Father, and outward as a servant to His people. Jesus said to find our lives, we must lose them. The enemy can't kill the man who has already died to himself! The enemy can't steal what we have surrendered and abandoned to the glory of God.

We were never meant to move in our own strength, power, or wisdom. Our weapons are mighty through God. Jesus said, *"'I am with you always, even to the end of the age.' Amen."* (Matthew 28:20b) Jesus promised that He would send the Holy Spirit, and He would be in us, giving us the power we need to be His witnesses to all the world. We accomplish God's work by His power according to His Word.

God reminded me of my purpose…my part in His story. My purpose was not to build His church. Jesus builds His church. My purpose was to preach His Word, in its entirety, from cover to cover. My purpose was to feed and care for His sheep. That is my place in this beautiful community we call the Body of Christ. It is all about the Lord Jesus. I live to follow the Lord, to obey the Lord. My purpose is to serve and glorify Him. I couldn't do it alone then, and I can't do it alone now. The good news is, I don't have to.

Chapter 5

Back to Work

"Then the Lord said to him: 'Go, return on your way to the Wilderness of Damascus; and when you arrive, anoint Hazael as king over Syria. Also you shall anoint Jehu the son of Nimshi as king over Israel. And Elisha the son of Shaphat of Abel Meholah you shall anoint as prophet in your place.'" (1 Kings 19:15-16)

A few years ago, my good friends Scott and Beverly Davey celebrated their 50th wedding anniversary. After fifty years together they can say one thing with certainty – that everything changes. They shed tears of joy in the good times and tears of sorrow when the storm clouds rolled in, but they weathered every season because they built their marriage and their lives on the Rock of Jesus Christ.

Elijah enjoyed the season of miraculous provision at the brook, but that season came to pass. It was time to move on to Zeraphath because God chose a Gentile widow and her son. (1 Kings 17). That season came to pass too, and it was time to move on to Mount Carmel. Carmel was the culmination of faith and perseverance, and it was a season of victory. However, that season also came to pass as it gave way to the season of testing. The good news was that the season of testing wouldn't last forever either. The season of testing gave way to the season of renewing and restoration.

The cave became a sweet place of refuge where Elijah could hide and commune with God. I know how tempting it is to want to stay in a place that feels safe. It couldn't have been easy for Elijah to leave the cave behind, but we're not meant to hide away from the world. God is our refuge and our hiding place, but at some point He strengthens us so He can raise us back up and send us back out.

God's story, our story: it's all about two things – the glory of God and the redemption of His people. God wasn't finished with Elijah. Mount Carmel was amazing, but that was an old chapter. New and exciting chapters awaited in Elijah's future with new mandates and new people along the way. There were new people who needed to hear from God.

Everything changes. It all comes to pass, but hang on because one thing is constant, a fixed point in our ever-changing lives. We anchor our lives in Jesus Christ, the Rock who never moves...our Immovable Mover. In Him we are like the tree planted by rivers of water, whose leaves never wither, a tree that bears fruit in every season to the glory of God.

It was time for me to go back to work. The season of hiding away was over. It all changes. God makes all things new. He keeps moving forward, but He is the same yesterday, today, and forever, our Ancient of

Days. He never changes. He was the same God on Mount Carmel as He was in the cave. God empowered Elijah to stand on the mountain, and God gave him the strength to leave the cave. God gave me the courage to embrace Western and Plains, and to stand back up. It all depended on God. It all still depends on God. It will forever depend on God, and that's good because God never fails.

We stand up. We find God's people, and we go back to work.

New Friends in Our Future

"And Elisha the son of Shaphat of Abel Meholah you shall anoint as prophet in your place." (1 Kings 19:16b)

Nothing is wasted when we surrender everything to the hand of God. It may look like Elijah lost valuable time by sitting under the tree or in the cave, but God used that time. He used it to reveal Himself. He used it to get Elijah's undivided attention. He also used it to unveil some new plans, not only for Elijah, but a young man named Elisha. Elijah would take what he learned in the cave and carry it into his future ministry for the remainder of his days. God also used Elijah's story to encourage and motivate me, thousands of years later. How's that for a life of meaning?!

It's been seventeen years since that season of depression, and I never want to go back under my broom tree, but I don't want to forget the lessons I learned while I was there. I carry them every day into my new beginnings, into my new chapters, and to my new friends awaiting me in my future.

"And he left the oxen and ran after Elijah, and said, 'Please let me kiss my father and my mother, and then I will follow you.' And he said to him, 'Go back again, for what have I done to you?' So Elisha turned back from him, and took a yoke of oxen and slaughtered them and boiled their flesh, using the oxen's equipment, and gave it to the people, and they ate. Then he arose and followed Elijah, and became his servant." (1 Kings 19:20-21)

God gave Elijah a special gift in this young man, Elisha. Elijah knew the cost of following God. He knew the risks, the sacrifices, the traps, but he also knew the power, the provision, and the victory. God would use Elisha to train a school of prophets, and an entire generation of prophets would be influenced by Elijah's legacy.

Mentoring someone God has chosen is a great honor, but Elijah wanted to make sure his protege understood what this call meant. "Think about it, Elisha, because once you follow me, there is no going back." There is a great cost to discipleship.

Elisha thought about it. He was all in. He gave everything he had in service to those around him, and he abandoned everything else as he followed his master. That kind of zeal becomes contagious, and it renewed Elijah's sense of purpose. We never find Elijah under the broom tree again after he met Elisha, though the attacks didn't end. Elijah would face his enemies again, more than once, but this time he didn't run. If Elijah had given up, he would never have met Elisha. He would have missed out.

My staff is full of young men and women I would never have met if I'd abandoned my call at Grace Church. I met Todd when he was a kid. He started dating one of the girls in my church, and they endured all kinds of storms; one being Todd losing his job. I hired him, and what started out as a job with radio evolved into a friendship. I baptized him in the Jordan River in Israel.

Landry is my worship leader. He's still in his twenties, and he answered the call to move hundreds of miles to Amarillo leaving everything else behind. My young staff – Todd, Landry, Doug, Chance, Asher, Mary, Tabitha, Nate – they're all my disciples, polite and faithful servants - just like Elisha; and they're my friends.

The Value of Old Friends

The old guys matter too. The young and the old, the new and the experienced, all work together to get the job done. Seventeen people originally started Grace Church, and some of those same friends are still with me. They know the struggles we faced to get to where we are now. They remember the

Sunday morning that I walked out of the church, between first and second service. I walked all the way to the street corner, and I knew if I took one more step, it would all end. I sat down on a railroad tie, and by God's grace and the unity of friends, I stood up, walked back inside, and preached second service. To this day, when I want to quit, I drive to that same spot and think about what would've happened if I had taken that step. I don't think on it too long because I don't want to think about what I would have missed out on. I wouldn't know so many people who are now precious members of my congregation. That faithfulness of my old friends, standing alongside me when I was weak, made all the difference.

Get connected. Don't do this alone. We can't do it alone. God designed us to be part of a covenant community all the way back in the Garden of Eden when He established the covenant between man and woman. We need each other.

Chapter 6

Practical Steps for Avoiding the Broom Tree

"Rejoice in the Lord always. Again I will say, rejoice! Let your gentleness be known to all men. The Lord is at hand. Be anxious for nothing, but in everything by prayer and supplication, with thanksgiving, let your requests be made known to God; and the peace of God, which surpasses all understanding, will guard your hearts and minds through Christ Jesus. Finally, brethren, whatever things are true, whatever things are noble, whatever things are just, whatever things are pure, whatever things are lovely, whatever things are of good report, if there is any virtue and if there is anything praiseworthy – meditate on these things. The things which you learned and received and heard and saw in me, these do, and the God of peace will be with you." (Philippians 4:4-9)

Joy in Christ dominates Paul's letter to the Philippian church. It's interesting to note that Paul wrote this letter while he was under house arrest in Rome. It would have been easy to write from a "woe is me" perspective, but Paul found the secret, even when he found himself under a broom tree so to speak. The joy of the Lord is our strength. He is the perfect mentor for giving advice on how to keep our heads above water when sorrows try to drown us.

- *Rejoice in Jesus.* He saved us! Our sins are erased! We're not going to hell! Nothing separates us from God. We will never be alone.
- *Let our gentleness be made known.* Kindness is contagious. Smile at people. Talk to them. Thank them. Kindness can change the atmosphere in a room. I write "be nice" on my hand every day to remind myself!
- *Stop worrying.* 80%-90% of the things we worry about never happen. Stop watching the news and open your Bible. Read Matthew 6. The birds and flowers worry about nothing because God takes care of them. It's easy to say, but hard to do. So, how do we do it? Do what the birds do. Sing! Praise God for what He has done. Worship God for who He is. Sing and speak, out loud, the praises of our Savior.
- *Pray!* The one small word that makes all the difference in a believer's life. Pray about everything, no matter how big or small.
- *"Finally brethren."* Become part of the local church. Connect with a church family. We're not made to do the work alone. Not even Jesus walked alone. His disciples were always with Him.
- *Filter what enters your mind.* There are shows I won't watch, songs I won't listen to, and

places I won't go because they will start my heart on the wrong path. Dwell on good things. As a man thinks in his heart, so is he.
- *Follow Godly Leaders.* Heed their instructions and imitate their lives.

Paul discovered the secret of lasting joy, and praise God he shared it with the rest of us. *"...for I have learned in whatever state I am, to be content: I know how to be abased, and I know how to abound. Everywhere and in all things I have learned both to be full and to be hungry, both to abound and to suffer need. **I can do all things through Christ who strengthens me.**" (Philippians 4:11-13, emphasis mine).*

Producing the Fragrance of Christ

"Now thanks be to God who always leads us in triumph in Christ, and through us diffuses the fragrance of His knowledge in every place. For we are to God the fragrance of Christ among those who are being saved and among those who are perishing."
(2 Corinthians 2:14-15)

People watch us more closely when trials turn up the heat in our lives. Heat enhances the aroma of what truly lies inside, like a pie baking in the oven. People are drawn to what smells good, and when we allow the Holy Spirit to work in our hearts, especially when the heat is dialed up, the fire will not smolder out. Instead, the fragrance of the Holy Spirit will permeate our being and be noticeable to others.

My worship leader uses an essential oil diffuser in his office, and the fragrance spreads everywhere. It never fails, when people walk in, they ask, "What's that smell?"

Hopefully we smell different than the rest of the world when we stand in line at the grocery store, or sit in the waiting room at the hospital, or at our workstations. Hopefully someone will ask, "What's that smell?"

We want people to see, hear, taste, touch, and smell Jesus in our lives. I still struggle with discouragement at times, but I know where to run when the heat is turned up. I've found my hiding place in Jesus Christ. I know how to draw near to those under the broom tree and administer the oil of the Holy Spirit because I've been there.

Chapter 7

Eye Has Not Seen, Ear Has Not Heard

"For now we see in a mirror, dimly, but then face to face. Now I know in part, but then I shall know just as I also am known." (1 Corinthians 13:12)

I love mountain top experiences. We all do. That's a God given desire that flows out of our yearning to dwell in God's presence and commune, unencumbered with Him. It allows small glimpses into the greater mountain that is soon to come.

Even after God ministered to Elijah in the cave, how tempting it must have been for him to gaze back at that mountain and think, "My glory days are over. The best has come and gone." No matter how we study, dissect, and interpret the events of 1 Kings 18, that is a fantastic story.

What could possibly top that story?

How about a whirlwind of fire that would carry him on into Heaven! As amazing as Mount Carmel was, it could never compare to that moment when God, Himself, decided it was time to bring Elijah home, and God honored him by sending him a special escort to his eternal destination. The moment the chariot arrived, Elijah never looked back. He laid down his friends, his earthly ministry, everything to be with God. Elijah didn't know that day was coming while he sat in the cave.

Yes! The whirlwind was great, but an even better moment awaited Elijah years and years into the future. Elijah stood with Jesus Christ on the Mount of Transfiguration. Everything in history had been leading to this moment. The birth of Israel, God's preservation of Israel, all of His prophecies and victories – all of it – had been about the Son of God. God used the kings, priests, prophets, and even ordinary men to carry the flame of hope that sparked to life when God promised to *"bruise the head" (Genesis 3:15)* of our enemy, until that flame found its resting place in Jesus Christ. Elijah stood on that mountain with Jesus, but the fire didn't fall that day. He stood with the Light of the Word. Everything about Elijah's life had been about this moment.

"Now after six days Jesus took Peter, James, and John his brother, led them up on a high mountain by themselves; and He was transfigured before them. His face shone like the sun, and His clothes became as white as the light. And behold, Moses and Elijah appeared to them, talking with Him. Then Peter answered and said to Jesus, 'Lord, it is good for us to be here; if You wish, let us make here three tabernacles: one for You, one for Moses, and one for Elijah.' While he was still speaking, behold, a bright cloud overshadowed them; and suddenly a voice came out of the cloud, saying, 'This is My beloved Son, in whom I am well pleased. Hear Him!' And when the disciples

heard it, they fell on their faces and were greatly afraid. But Jesus came and touched them and said, 'Arise, and do not be afraid.' When they had lifted up their eyes, they saw no one but Jesus only." (Matthew 17:1-8)

In the presence of Christ's glory, the limitations between heaven and earth, between time and space, between past, present, and future disappeared as the Ancient of Days who was, and is, and is to come was revealed.

Elijah stood up for God's Word. Jesus was the Word made flesh. Elijah was a great prophet of God. Jesus was the fulfillment and realization of every prophecy given. It had to be more than Elijah even knew to hope for because Elijah's story was written to the eternal glory of Jesus Christ.

The Cross Had to Come

"From that time Jesus began to show His disciples that He must go to Jerusalem, and suffer many things from the elders and chief priests and scribes, and be killed, and be raised on the third day. Then Peter took Him aside and began to rebuke Him, saying, 'Far be it from You, Lord; this shall not happen to You!' But He turned and said to Peter, 'Get behind Me, Satan! You are an offense to Me, for you are not mindful of the things of God, but the things of men.' Then Jesus said to His disciples, 'If anyone desires to come after Me,

*let him deny himself, and take up his cross, and follow
Me. For whoever desires to save his life will lose it,
but whoever loses his life for My sake will find it. For
what profit is it to a man if he gains the whole world,
and loses his own soul? Or what will a man give in
exchange for his soul? For the Son of Man will come
in the glory of His Father with His angels, and then He
will reward each according to his works. Assuredly, I
say to you, there are some standing here who shall
not taste death till they see the Son of Man coming in
His kingdom.'" (Matthew 16:21-28)*

Love is the chief principle that governs the Kingdom
of God. God so LOVED the world. Jesus didn't come
to condemn the world, but to save the world through
Himself. (John 3:17) That meant carrying a cross. He
set His face like flint to fulfill the purpose of His life. He
refused to allow anything or anyone to distract Him for
the work He was sent here to complete. And praise
God, He did complete the work.

Jesus clearly saw that day because He is God
the Son, Alpha and Omega, from Everlasting to
Everlasting. It's why He embraced the cross, despis-
ing its shame. (Hebrews 12:2) He knew temporary
suffering would end and give way to His eternal glory,
and it was worth it. Our eternal salvation was worth
the agony to Jesus.

Jesus carried His cross. If the disciples wanted to
follow Jesus, they too would have to carry their cross.

So will we. Don't let anyone tell you Christianity is the key to an easy life. Christianity is the key to eternal and abundant life; filled with mountains and valleys; filled with crosses and crowns.

God's desire that every soul be saved overrides our desire to be comfortable. God didn't spare His own Son, but allowed Him to suffer because His heart was on the eternal redemption of mankind. God sent Jesus to redeem the world.

Our God lives and moves with this eternal perspective in mind because He is from everlasting to everlasting. God sees the entire picture, not just the snippets we see as time moves on. He has the clear and eternal view. We're created in God's image, and He placed eternity in our hearts. Our souls live forever, and it will either be in eternal life or eternal death.

Elljah's suffering was temporary. It came to pass. Momentary testing would give way to everlasting reward. Elijah didn't know the big picture, but we do. The Word of God promised *"that the sufferings of this present time are not worthy to be compared with the glory which shall be revealed in us." (Romans 8:18)*

We know how it ends. We know where we're going.

"Eye has not seen, nor ear heard, Nor have entered into the heart of man the things which God has prepared for those who love Him." (1 Corinthians 2:9)

Jesus warned us. Trouble would come, but in that same breath He gave us the promise of all promises.

"I HAVE OVERCOME THE WORLD!" Jesus is the big picture. We set our face towards Him.

The Light did overcome the darkness. It did from the beginning of time, when God said, "let there be light." And, it will again when Jesus makes His home among His people. There will be no need for light in that Holy City because the Lord God will be its light. (Revelation 22:5)

"Let not your heart be troubled; you believe in God, believe also in Me. In My Father's house are many mansions; if it were not so, I would have told you. I go to prepare a place for you. And if I go and prepare a place for you, I will come again and receive you to Myself; that where I am, there you may be also. And where I go you know, and the way you know. Thomas said to Him, 'Lord, we do not know where You are going, and how can we know the way?' Jesus said to him, 'I am the way, the truth, and the life. No one comes to the Father except through Me.'"(John 14:1-6)